interlude

the sea quills

ISBN-13: 978-0615908953
ISBN-10: 0615908950

Cover art: "Garden" by Marilyn Coyne, 2013. Courtesy of the artist.

Cover by Joleene Naylor.

Book design: Elizabeth King Humphrey.

Southern Salon Press.

In memory of Blonnie Bunn Wyche,
our southern sister.

About the Sea Quills

The Sea Quills took shape in June 2011 when **Charlene Pollano** moved to the Wilmington area and joined the North Carolina Writers' Network. She met **Christine Parker** at a NCWN meeting and they chatted about forming a writing and critique group. **Teri Meadowcroft** contacted them after seeing their ad posted on the NCWN website. An organizational meeting was held and the Sea Quills was born. A month later **Blonnie Bunn Wyche** and **Georgia Ann Mullen** signed on. Meetings were held at Blonnie's house until she passed away in May 2012. **Nancy Gadzuk** is the group's newest member.

The Sea Quills are always on the lookout for talented writers who benefit from the camaraderie of a critique group and who share the core belief that how one gives feedback can be a profound influence on a writer's creative life.

The Sea Quills have served as regional representatives for the NCWN since March 2012, organizing and facilitating monthly presentations and informal meetings to assist area writers in networking with others. All members live in the greater Wilmington/Cape Fear region.

Contents

Game Time
Nancy Gadzuk

All eyes were on Deirdre when she walked into the room. She hated times like this. Those stares, what they were thinking behind their glassy eyes, always made her uncomfortable. Wet circles began forming under her armpits.

Great. Now they could make fun of her hygiene as well as her clothes, her chewed nails.

The room was quiet a second too long; then Jed stood up. "Glad you could make it, Dee." No one called her Dee. He opened the refrigerator and pulled out a can of cheap beer. He handed it to her and she nodded thanks, took a short sip of the watery liquid. It wasn't even cold. Ugh, how could they drink that shit when there were so many decent beers out there?

Conversation started again. Larry launched into a monologue that left Deirdre dazed and everyone else entertained. She'd probably interrupted him by showing up. He finally stopped to take a breath and everyone except Deirdre laughed. He must have gotten to the punch line.

Tammy and Britt held their bottles up to Larry in a mock salute and clicked their bottles together.

They were drinking an India Pale Ale from Deirdre's favorite microbrewery. Then Deirdre noticed that everyone was drinking good beer–Larry, Jed, the rest of them.

What the fuck?

interlude

Deirdre imagined pouring her warm beer into the big bowl of chips on the coffee table, or better yet, down Jed's back. It was the first time she smiled all day.

Instead, she walked to the bar sink and tipped her can high, watching the foamy liquid swirl down the drain. She caught Jed staring at her as she opened the refrigerator and got herself a bottle of IPA. She took a long draught from the bottle and stared back. Much better.

So this was the "man cave" Jed talked about incessantly at work. She looked around. Testosterone oozed from the black leather couches, the big flat panel TV, the dartboard hanging on the wall.

She'd been included inadvertently, she'd assumed, in an email inviting the staff to his house for potluck and the game on Sunday. Deirdre hated football, thought she'd leave before the game started.

But her New Year's resolution had been to get out of her own skin more, to act normal. This was an opportunity for her to at least try. Even her therapist would be pleased.

Her clothes were, as usual, all wrong for the afternoon. She'd worn dark slacks and a twin set. Everyone else was in jeans and a logo team shirt.

"Who's playing?" This was wrong. She realized that even as the words were coming out. The looks ranged from incredulous to pitying. Well, screw them. They probably had no idea what was happening politically halfway around the world, let alone halfway across the city, if it didn't carry a football team banner.

The silence lasted an instant too long. Tammy rolled her eyes for Britt's benefit, and Britt barely stifled a chuckle. That did it.

Deirdre would play her own game.

"Hey!" Deirdre's voice was jovial. "Who wants to play darts before the game?" Her co-workers looked at her. They'd never heard that upbeat voice. No one spoke.

"I said, who wants to play darts?" This time her tone was different. Tammy shifted uneasily in the leather loveseat. Jed stood up. No one spoke.

Deirdre grabbed the darts from the corkboard. They were expensive darts: heavy, weighted just right. The kind she liked. At least Jed had picked those well. She aimed for him first. He dropped silently to the shag carpeting.

Were they all really moving in slow motion, or was it her adrenalin? Deirdre was able to aim slowly, carefully, accurately. Soon she'd used all the darts, and the room was quiet.

She stepped over Britt's body on her way to the refrigerator. She wanted to grab a couple of beers to take home.

She might watch the football game after all.

I've Moved
Christine Parker

Destiny tugged
A different theatre.
Scripts started,
Props prepared.
Casting call,
Parts played.

Playback performances,
Troupers faraway.
Hearts hankering,
Tears teasing.
Shared stages
Forever set.

Protagonist enters,
Curtains ascend.
Silver screen dreams,
Footlights beam.
Author, actor,
Merging screens.

I Almost Remember
Charlene Pollano

The North Church clock chimes four o'clock. I peer into the small mirror mounted on the back of my office door, and an unfamiliar face stares back. I hung the mirror for female clients to check the condition of their makeup after a therapy session, repair the wounds of having done battle with their feelings. I am surprised how many men do the same. And now, me. I brush my bangs to the side, tuck the auburn shoulder-length hair behind my ears, and make a face at the purple shadows under my eyes, harbingers of my own recent struggles with past specters.

Psychotherapy is such a strange way to make a living. Being so involved in people's lives for a brief amount of time, then watching them leave to begin anew the business of life. A psychologist once said much of therapy was simply being curious about the minutiae of people's day-to-day lives. As a therapist, I feel as though I have devoted a lifetime to getting a front-row view of emotional pain. I rarely know where my clients end up, or how. It's such unfinished business, as with my childhood friend, Tess. No closure, like many aspects of life. I think how funny it is that, in fiction, life always comes to a point. Maybe it's why I bury myself in books so much…there are clear beginnings and endings.

I head down the narrow hallway toward the waiting room. The pumpkin-colored, wide pine floor creaks as I pick my way toward the figure sitting there.

interlude

"Hey, Dr. B, how's it going?" Meg says, with a big grin on her pale face. She springs up from the waiting room couch, sprints down the hall, and puts her arm around my shoulder as she looks down at me.

"Hey, Meg. New hairdo?" I study her cropped head with its spiked, dirty blond hair. She whisks by me into the office, heads right for the sofa opposite my chair, and plops down, stretching out her wiry, five-eight frame.

"Yeah, what do you think?" she says, studying my face. She turns to show me the long tail of hair left in the back, pulling it out from under her warm-up jacket, which she procured by means of her "five-finger discount," as she calls it.

Meg is a master of detection, probably had to be in her house, so I am careful to keep a poker face readily available, a skill I have developed in my years as a therapist. "I don't know, let me study it for a while," I say, as I watch Meg's legs twitch and bounce.

Today, the "hyper" Meg is here as opposed to the "somber" one. Since I handle her active self more easily, I settle into my chair armed with a small amount of optimism. She reminds me of bike rides, Tess in front of me, hands in the air.

Meg jettisons off the couch into the desk chair. Sitting arrow-straight, she reaches around to her right with both arms, twisting the top of her torso, grabs the back of the seat, and pulls, making a cracking noise with her back. She repeats the action to her left, bounds back to the couch, and resumes her sprawled posture.

I observe the ritual, not flinching this time, having witnessed this exercise in back-cracking numerous times. We have decided it's her body limbering up for the business of therapy.

She flashes a smile and says, "Time's up, you have to tell me."

14

"Okay, I kind of like it, but it makes your face look a little harsh."

She beams. "Well, just means the outside matches the inside. Plus, it's easier for me when I run track. Cuts down on wind resistance. And best of all, my old man hates it. Says I look like a goddamned dyke."

"Mmmm, how is Dad these days, still angry about you coming here?"

"Who gives a shit? It's court-ordered, so he can't say much. He doesn't bug me about this because he's afraid I might talk."

I feel a sudden heaviness in the air as the brief moments of optimism fade away, and the words "afraid" and "talk" reverberate in my ears. My own words force their way out.

"What do you mean, Meg?" I try to say more, but stop myself when I hear the halting way these words drip out.

"Nothing. Hey, I wanted to tell you about something that happened this week at school. Do you want to hear it?" She settles farther into the corner of the couch, legs still jumping away, sneakers swaying back and forth. Suddenly she leaps up, grabs the watering can from its corner, and begins to water the sprawling philodendron plants in the windows.

"I'd like to hear why your father is afraid of you talking." These words emerge intact, but my body has begun a quiet shivering.

Meg finishes with the watering and wedges herself back into the corner of the couch. "I said it was nothing. He just likes me to keep my mouth shut about private family stuff." She begins to drum the arm of the couch, always keeping her eyes on mine. "Do you want to hear about school or not?"

"If that's what you want." I grip a pen and notepad, hoping to hide the shaking.

15

"I got in a fight with this asshole senior boy who called me a name, a filthy one I wouldn't even tell you. I lost it. Not on him, though. On the wall outside the cafeteria. The bad news is the wall was cement block, the good news is it's not broken." She holds up her swollen left hand, which ranges in color from yellow to purple.

"And the boy?" I ask.

"Suspended. Sexual harassment. Not what I wanted to tell you, though." She leans her head onto the back of the couch and gazes up at the ceiling.

I look at Meg's upturned face, gaunt and still as she assembles her energy to dive into the abyss, drag out what's there, turn it over, and attempt to deal with it. The face of a ghost, a form without a soul.

Tess looked the same way as she floated past me in the hallway in high school, years after the night that changed our lives forever. I felt sick to my stomach every time I saw her, found ways to avoid seeing her between classes. The identical queasy feeling erupts now, just as it has for the last few months of Meg's therapy.

One of the hardest things for me to learn as a therapist is that people have a right to hang onto their problems. The second hardest is when they do decide to let go of them, it takes as long as it takes. Internal systems have their own pace.

Meg meets my blue eyes with her brown ones. She searches, looking for some reassurance that, this time, someone will hear what she says. A recognizable torture rushes headlong at me—that lack of understanding in our youths, when we really need it. How many times in my life have I said, "If I only knew then what I know now?"

"You know the thing you say I have, the PTSD something?" she whispers.

"Yes, post-traumatic stress disorder is what it's called."

"Yeah, whatever. Anyway, two other girls in my survivors' group have you as a shrink. We found out the other night when one of 'em was talking about the traumatic stress thing and mentioned you. You really like working with people like us, huh?" She begins to crack her knuckles, one at a time, on her good right hand. I flinch at each snap as though a gunshot has split the air.

"I guess you could say the local judges recognize me as a sort of specialist in the area of sexual assault because I've had a lot of clients who have given me experience." The words penetrate the air quietly and merge with the sputtering of the fire. "Meg, were you going to tell me something?"

"I don't know," she says, as she leans forward, placing her head in her hands, elbows on her knees. She gazes into the fire. "I can't sleep at night."

"What makes me think that isn't what you wanted to tell me?"

As I say this, Meg lifts her bristly head, smiles one of her unnerving, almost hostile smiles.

I lean forward to meet her gaze. "Remember the space suit analogy I told you about? I promise I won't make you take your space suit off on this alien planet until you believe you can breathe without it. Okay?"

Just then, another log in the fireplace rolls over, sending sparks crackling up its walls. My nerves feel like they're crackling along my inner torso too, but I hold Meg's gaze because I know if I flinch, she will detect it.

"I heard my grandfather might be getting out in six months," she says. Tiny beads of sweat appear on her upper lip, and the legs cease to bounce. "That's why I can't sleep." She collapses into the cushions. "By the way," she adds, "I like the 'House of Cards' analogy better than the space suit one."

interlude

I can't help but smile. "Explain why," I say, letting her get away with the change of topic this time.

"I'll do better, I'll show you." She pulls a deck of cards from her jacket pocket and shuffles them with the elegance of a Las Vegas blackjack dealer, bruised hand notwithstanding. "How to productively waste your time in study hall," she says.

She draws a card from the deck and begins to build her house across the sea chest that serves as a coffee table between us. Each card is placed with precision, layer upon layer, until she has five layers resting one atop the other.

"Well, I'm the house of cards." Holding her breath, she lays the final card on top of the pyramid. "You can touch the top part, and you can even build onto it, but if you get anywhere near the foundation…" She flicks her thumb and forefinger against the bottom layer and smiles at me as the cards flutter and tumble in a heap.

The above selection is an excerpt from I Almost Remember, *Charlene Pollano's novel in progress.*

Lonely
Christine Parker

I thought I was lonely so I got a dog.
I thought the dog was lonely so I got a cat.
Now I'm no longer lonely,
I'm just out of my mind.

My family thought I was lonely.
My sister, my mother, my brother
Didn't want me to be lonely.
They drove miles to visit
So I wouldn't be alone.
I'm not lonely,
I'm out of my mind.

When a big hurricane came to visit
So did my family.
My mother, my brother, my sister and all their children.
A little wind here, a lot of blowing there,
The top of my head flew off.

My daughter didn't want me to be lonely.
She moved in for an indefinite stay.
The dog, the cat, the family visits,
I wasn't lonely. I went for professional help.

interlude

The therapist was new to town.
She said she was so happy to meet me,
"A nice, interesting person,"
So she won't be lonely.
I can't seem to really lose my mind.

I walked up the beach and down the beach.
I looked at the people and watched the waves.
A lonely looking person started to walk towards me.
It was more than I could bear.
I screamed at him,
"Stay away, I'm out of my mind."

The hot season is passing.
I promise never to be lonely again.
My other sister is moving to my town.
Says she doesn't want to be lonely.
I'm joyful, I'm delirious.
This will be the last nudge.
I am going, going, gone out of my mind.

Worse than Dead
Georgia Ann Mullen

Don't the dead stay dead? Last winter I saw August's snow-covered grave. Read her name and the year she died—1851—scratched into a wooden cross. Now it's spring, and still I weep. Grieve in quiet fury. Because I know, deep down, gentle August will not walk this earth again.

I reread the telegram handed to me moments ago.

COME TO OBERLIN
I'VE SEEN AUGUST

Lucy Manning! She should know better than to send this claptrap message. She saw the bleeding hole in August's chest. I want to slap her. Scream, "You did not see August because August is dead!"

She's cold as a wagon tire! Killed by her own hand rather than be hauled back to the slave plantation she ran from fourteen years ago.

I stuff the telegram inside my pocket and hurry through Buffalo's busy Erie Canal Harbor. My quiet lunch on Commercial Slip is shattered.

"What's it say, Tessie?" Talbot, the boy who brought the telegram, runs beside me. "Bad news?"

"Shut it! Ain't bad news. Ain't good. Just a mistake."

"A mistake telegram?"

"Skip it." I press my hand against the paper in my pocket. "And don't say a word about it to anybody."

"But if Grandma asks—"

"Not a word to Wixumlee!" She's the last person I want reading Lucy's message. "Go back to the tavern. I'll be home for supper."

I leave work early but not for supper. Sneaking upstairs, I pull my corduroy satchel from under my bed and pack it with Kentucky blue jeans, flannel shirts and an extra sweater—not usual girl garments, but clothes I've worn for years and that feel comfortable on my tall, big-boned frame. Most folks in the small town where I grew up got tired of trying to embarrass me back into dresses. None of the roughneck sailors and canawlers hanging around this Buffalo port give a hoot. Some strangers look cross-eyed at me, wondering if I'm a boy or a girl. I don't let it bother me. I know who I am. A girl who wears pants.

I open my locked box and stuff all the money into my pockets. A lump rises in my throat. August, alive? I swallow hard. Impossible. She's dead. Dead because I couldn't save her.

I was three years old when August showed up spent, heavy with child, and begging for water at our back door. Ma took her in, but August went from one life of toil and trouble into another. Sweating in a hot kitchen, cooking for Ma's boarders. Fending off Pa's rough hands, turning away from his whiskey breath. Fearing for the white man's child she gave birth to a month later in the tiny room off our kitchen. She named that long, skinny babe Beany. Together we grew up in August's kitchen, me tormenting her quiet daughter like a younger sister.

I snap my satchel shut and take several deep breaths. In a fit of spite, Pa turned slave catchers on August. Now she's dead. Dead!

I close my bedroom door, tread lightly down the stairs and peek into the kitchen. No one's there. I grab some apples and a loaf of walnut bread cooling on the table and drop them into my grip. I ease out the back door, braced for the long trip from Buffalo, New York to Oberlin, Ohio.

***

Slumped in my stagecoach seat en route to Cleveland, I worry about not leaving a note. If I lied and said I went to visit Ma, Wixumlee would get in touch with her. I can't tell the truth—that I went looking for August 'cause Lucy thinks she saw her alive. Besides being ridiculous, it would stir up a pile of problems.

After the battle on the canal towpath that took August's life, me, Beany, and my brother, Cooper, fled our hometown of Seneca Falls and rode the Erie Canal west to Black Rock. In that tough port north of Buffalo, I was no longer the scrappy rebel who settled fights with my fists. The slave catchers' brutality had changed me into a sniveling coward. Beany was in worse shape. She was sick, silent and nearly soulless after yanking the bluestone knife out of her mama's chest. One day, while I hawked boat tickets on the Black Rock towpath, a fancy-dressed "white" woman picked up Beany and carried her to the Black Pole Tavern. I followed, reluctantly, fearfully, into Wixumlee's domain. While she coddled Beany into recovering from the violent loss of her mama, Wixumlee—an octoroon, as I heard her called— bullied me into joining in the militant deeds of her abolition army.

It took me four months of gruesome mistakes to begin rebuilding the confidence I lost after that towpath fight with slave catchers. One of those mistakes was losing a slave baby over a waterfall—a wound deep inside me that will never heal. Another was trying to drown Nicky Pappo, Wixumlee's number one spy. It was one stumble after another, but I finally won Wixumlee's trust. Now she buys my clothes, feeds me and even pays me as a seventeen-year-old soldier in her abolition army.

Wixumlee took me under her wing, but it was Beany, then thirteen, who captured her heart. The woman considers herself the girl's mama now and won't give her up. Wixumlee doesn't give up. Anything. Ever. And Beany accepts Wixumlee as her ma, too. I can't toss her world—tell her Lucy turned lunatic and thinks she saw August alive. Beany accepts her mama's death. I won't rake her ragged with rumors.

Fingering the telegram in my pocket, I stare out the stagecoach window at leafless trees as brown and bare as my own grim thoughts.

In Cleveland I board a train going south. Hunched on a hard seat, I pull Lucy's telegram from my coat pocket and read it again. She saw August. I snort. Impossible. August was bloody, lifeless, when we left her on the towpath. With help from Cooper's canawler mates, we beat the slave catchers, but we couldn't save August. I'm taking this trip to Oberlin for one reason: to blame Lucy for shattering the calm that finally settled over my life.

Me and Lucy didn't jump in as friends. A year older than me, she was Miss Priss with a lawyer father, and I was tough Tess with a drunken pa. Lucy aimed for Oberlin College. I itched to hop a cargo and travel the Erie Canal. It wasn't 'til we worked together on *The Lily*, a temperance and women's rights paper, that we started to tolerate each other's dreams—and even like each other. Lucy's my friend now, but she can still burrow under my skin like a tick.

A skinny man with a fat cough lights a cigar and blows smoke over the top of my head. The elderly woman next to me covers her nose with her hand. I open the window a couple inches, and she nods gratefully. I watch a line of gray ash sift through the opening.

Friends or not, Lucy's gonna turn to smoke when I get to town.

***

The train drops me off at the edge of Oberlin, a small town southwest of Cleveland. There's no depot, just a gray structure with a plain sign naming it Russia House. Walking up Main Street, I cross a narrow creek and come to a large square, crisscrossed by paths, with a cluster of multistory buildings filling one quadrant.

A dark-skinned man with a braided ponytail sweeps the sidewalk outside a grocery. He tells me where to find the Klinger house near Plum Creek, where Lucy rents a room. She's walking up the path toward the front door when I sneak up behind her.

"Lucy!"

Her shriek is small payment for shaking my serenity.

"Can't you extend a civil greeting?" She taps her fingers into the little hollow at the base of her neck. "You didn't acknowledge my communication. Now you—"

"Stop! I'm here. I'm tired. But you dang well better believe I want to talk. How can you say—?"

"Not here." She pulls me down the street. "I have no privacy here. We'll talk in the Park."

College Park turns out to be the large, muddy square in the center of town, nearly bare of trees and fair game for Lake Erie's icy fingers. Lucy points to the Elm and says the tree marks where the founding fathers stopped twenty years ago to hack out of the wilderness the only school in the country that accepts women and people of color. The reasons Lucy fought hard to attend Oberlin College.

I stretch my coat collar up over my neck and yank my knit cap down over my ears. Early April in Oberlin is as miserable as early

interlude

April in Buffalo. Looking around, I can't believe my eyes. I never saw—or read about—or saw a picture of—a plainer town in all my life.

"Don't they sell paint here?" Across the street, simple frame houses are nailed together with white boards.

"Of course they sell paint. They sell white paint."

I can only shake my head. "Tell me where you think you saw August."

"I don't think—I saw her. In Maysville, Kentucky. I went with a group to speak against slavery."

The name Maysville rings a bell—a loud one. It's home base for the slave catcher, Beau Maas. My heart giddy-ups. Word came this winter through the underground about Maas crossing the Ohio River and chasing runaways as far north as Columbus, in the middle of the state.

"This woman. What was she doing?"

"Loading a buckboard. Sacks of flour, sugar, beans."

"How close were you?"

"Two stores away."

"Did she see you?"

Two female students, buttoning black coats over gray dresses, pass us. The bonnet of one flips off in the wind, showing hair parted down the middle, stretched tight and spun into a doughnut-size roll at the base of her neck. Lucy, as if in spite, has piled her hair atop her head and encouraged wispy curls to dangle near her ears and over her collar. The skirt of her sky blue dress swirls below a dark red woolen jacket. There's a gust of wind, and Lucy clutches the yellow scarf puffed below her chin to her throat.

I stamp my foot. "Cripes, Luce, did she see you?"

Lucy looks across the square. "She never looked up. Just kept her eyes on the goods and the ground."

I swallow hard. "Like a slave."

Lucy raises her gaze to mine. "Like a slave."

The above selection is an excerpt from Worse than Dead, *Georgia Ann Mullen's novel in progress.*

Bad Math
Jeanmarie "Teri" Meadowcroft

Look, there's one of my legs
on the kitchen floor.
My head lies in the bedroom,
And my arm fell behind the couch.
Most of my hair came out in the shower
And my teeth dropped out in bed.

I cannot seem to put myself
Back together today.

I have been reduced to
Fractions and
These fractions don't add up.
It's bad math.
Bad math, all around.

Nectar
Nancy Gadzuk

Lureen stirred the pitcher of sugar water and smiled. Oh, her hummingbirds surely did love this sweet nectar! And the bees: some days she believed they swarmed under the trees in the back yard, just waiting for her to come outside so they could drink.

"Lureen! Hurry it up with my lunch!" Her husband scowled from his lounge chair in front of the TV. It was the first he'd spoken to her all day.

Well, he'd just have to wait. Her winged friends were going to get fed first.

She carried the pitcher out on the porch. Goodness, the air was alive today! Her little friends must be hungry. She filled the hummingbird feeders carefully so the nectar wouldn't drip around the base. Then she poured some nectar into open saucers so the bees could drink from them and leave the hummingbirds to their own feeders.

The air crackled with anticipation; she could feel it. She sensed a sphere of movement, of tiny wings, circling under the peach trees near the fence.

"Dammit, woman! I want my lunch."

She hurried back to the kitchen. She'd made Willard a meatloaf sandwich slathered with red currant jelly. She poured him a tall glass of sweet tea.

"I'll just take it outside so y'all can set on the porch and eat. There's fresh peach pie, too. Still warm."

interlude

Willard grunted and scratched his crotch as he shuffled toward the door. "'Bout time it's ready."

She looked at him: his grey stubble, his hard eyes.

"Oh, it's ready," she said.

She set the tray on the table and admired the border of purple yarrow and yellow coreopsis that flowered alongside the porch.

Willard grabbed the sandwich and started wolfing it down. Lureen watched for a few minutes. Then, satisfied, she went indoors, went into the kitchen to wash dishes.

She never heard a thing over the sound of the running water, she would say later. Not a cry, not the thud of his chair falling over.

Not the buzz of a thousand swarming bees.

Etiquette Misfits
Christine Parker

The use of cell phones in public places is becoming a problem. One can't go anywhere without hearing someone on a cell chatting about what he had for breakfast or another yakking about the prep work for his colonoscopy. Phew, that guy had diarrhea coming out of more than one orifice.

Did these people leave their manners in a cave? *Who are their people?*

Why does someone think they are so important they can make a call in a restaurant and scream into the phone while others are trying to eat a lovely meal? Or pick up their cell phones when I am with them in the car, the store, wherever and carry on as if I am not even there. Making me look like a plastic blow-up doll—deaf, dumb and idiotic. Am I dead meat to this dead beat?

What about the lady who answers her cell phone in church? She leans down in the pew and makes plans for lunch. Then there are the kids who text while driving. Duh, some of them won't live to see their twentieth birthdays.

Cell phone jerks are equal opportunity offenders. They come in all ages, races, nationalities and occupations. You can find them in restaurants, on public transportation, in theaters, churches, public restrooms and while hiking.

So what can we do about it? Banish these jerks to an island for etiquette misfits? I actually hand the offenders a card. It's business size and shows a person on a train using a cell phone. The rest of the passengers glare at him. If glares could be daggers, he would be dead.

My previous attempts to curb obnoxious behavior have not been as mature. When shopping and annoyed by some ding dong prattling on, I sang out loud while walking up and down the aisles. Jingle Bells sounds a little funny at Easter.

Sometimes I am circumspect. I went into my therapist's waiting room and saw a woman smoking an e-cigarette and her husband on his cell phone. I became undone. Pointing to the two Neanderthals, I frantically waved at the poisonous vapors shouting *"verboten...*get out." Then the therapist opened the door and boom—committed me.

The Minister's Wife
Jeanmarie "Teri" Meadowcroft

Paul knew certain members of his congregation thought he'd made a mistake. He'd married his office assistant, a woman twelve years his junior, after a four-month courtship. While he didn't regret the marriage, the church elders made it clear his parishioners didn't want to see their minister behaving like a lovesick teenager.

So Paul resisted the urge to look out his study window at his wife of two months. He knew Victoria remained in her garden even as twilight fell over the frozen land. He wanted to knock on the glass and wave her inside. But Anna Bahr needed his full attention.

Anna had come to plan her father's funeral. She held a wrinkled tissue in one hand and her husband's hand in the other. Evening shadows encroached on the study and cast purple smudges beneath Anna's eyes. She leaned against the strong shoulder of her husband, Rick.

"My mother needed my help," Anna said. "I should have done more."

"You needed to be home with your children," Paul said.

For the past two months, Paul had watched Anna struggle to balance her roles as wife, mother and daughter as her father underwent chemotherapy.

Anna's chin quivered and she sniffled. Paul handed her a box of tissues. She clutched the box with whitened fingers, but made no move to take any. Tears ran down her cheeks.

Rick put his arm around his wife and spoke soothing words in her ear, words Paul could not hear. The tension in Anna's shoulders eased.

Anna drew a deep breath and let it out. "I can't give the eulogy," Anna said. "I'm no good with words."

"Would your brother be willing to do it?" Paul asked.

Anna pulled a tissue from the box and worried it. "I think so."

Paul got up and turned on a small side lamp to counter the growing shadows. When he returned to his chair, he shifted it so he could see Victoria through the window.

She knelt on the hard-packed earth and worked a hand rake over the ground with little apparent success. She paused and her gaze focused on something beyond Paul's sight.

He had met Victoria the day of her father's funeral, eight years ago. Victoria was fifteen, but Paul guessed her to be in her early twenties that day. Her dress and low heels made her look older.

He remembered the way the barrette caught her hair up on her head. Stray locks fell on her graceful neck, and his gaze returned there again and again. When he learned her real age, he was stunned. It was an inauspicious start to their relationship.

They met when she was fifteen, had sex when she was eighteen, went out on their first date when she was twenty-two. To Paul, sometimes their entire relationship felt like a series of mistakes only marriage could set right.

"I'm just so tired, Reverend Paul," Anna said. "And my mother is worn out. I don't know about readings, or music or any of that."

"Maybe the reading from Matthew 11:25 would be appropriate," he said. "I'm sure you're familiar with it. It says, *Come to me, all you who are weary and burdened, and I will give you rest.*"

"I think my mother would like that." Anna looked to Rick. "Don't you?"

"Yes," Rick said. "I think she would."

From the adjoining kitchen, Paul heard the back door open. Some of the tension left his body. Victoria had come inside. He glanced at the clock. Five-thirty.

34

Anna stirred. "Oh, I had no idea it'd gotten so late." She returned the tissue box to his desk and gathered her coat.

"Please don't worry," Paul said. "We have time."

"Could you pick the rest of the readings?" Anna said. "I've got to get back to the children."

"Of course," Paul said. "Who's with them now?"

Rick answered. "My sister. She's good with them."

Anna tried to wipe away her smeared mascara. Then, by some invisible signal, she and Rick rose together. Paul extended his hand to Rick.

"Thank you, Reverend."

Rick held Anna's coat as she slipped her arms into it. His hand lingered, and he rubbed her back. She shot him a grateful look. To Paul, this small gesture seemed instinctive. He wondered when, in a marriage, that instinct developed.

Anna headed into the kitchen. Paul hung back. "How long have you and Anna been married?" he asked Rick.

Rick gazed up at the ceiling. "It'll be nineteen years this July." The deep groove between Rick's eyebrows eased. "Hard to believe it's been that long."

Paul glanced into the other room. Anna spoke and Victoria nodded from time to time. A frown settled on his wife's face and she bit her lip. Dealing with people she didn't know well, during their most difficult moments, was new to her. She would learn, he thought.

She learned how to run the church office when he gave her the job at sixteen. She would learn the role of minister's wife as well.

"And you, you're still a newlywed," Rick said.

Paul's face grew hot, and he gave the other man an awkward smile. He never knew which of his parishioners disapproved and which ones believed it was none of their business. Rick appeared to fall into the latter camp.

Rick smiled and clapped Paul on the shoulder. "Don't worry. It gets easier, Reverend. But women are always a bit of a puzzle."

Paul gave a weak laugh. "Boy, isn't that the truth."

He remembered the night when Victoria came to him in his study, five years ago. He'd been reading and enjoying a beer when she knocked. Her eyes appeared bloodshot and raw, as if she'd been crying. She paced the room and tried to explain what had upset her, but in the end, all he got from her was that it involved an argument at home.

Paul's head buzzed with his second beer and, when she kissed him, he made no effort to resist. The light floral scent of her hair and skin intoxicated him. He followed her lead. She slid the straps of her sundress from her shoulders, lay back on the couch and pulled him with her.

She lifted her hips to allow his hands access when he sought it. He remembered the satin feel of her skin as he pushed her dress up her thighs. He thought he'd died when she guided him between her legs with her hand. He took her there, on the couch.

No, that wasn't quite right. She had given herself to him that night, with an eagerness that, when he recalled it, seemed closer to desperation than desire. The memory still made his stomach churn and filled him with a longing that he refused to examine. She had never given herself with such abandonment since.

The morning after, he got down on his knees and begged God for forgiveness. He'd never before slept with a member of his congregation, let alone an eighteen-year-old girl.

Had he hurt her? Made her afraid? He couldn't bring himself to ask. He begged her forgiveness and she granted it easily, as if relieved to know he wouldn't expect more of her. They never spoke of that night again.

Paul ushered Rick into the kitchen, and then he and Victoria walked the couple to the door. Cold night air rushed in to dispel the warmth of the house.

Once the Bahrs' car departed, Paul put his hand to the small of Victoria's back. "It's warmer in the kitchen," he said.

She stepped away before his hand could settle. "I need to check the meat loaf."

Paul followed Victoria into the buttery yellow light. Her loose hair hid the curve of her neck he loved. He longed to walk up behind her, brush her hair aside and put his lips to her skin.

"Weren't you cold out there?" he asked. "Without a coat?"

She threw him a curious glance. "Cold?"

"In the garden," he said.

She shrugged. "It doesn't bother me."

Paul once asked her why she worked her plot of dirt when it was far too early to plant anything. He assumed it was her way of making herself at home. She'd had a garden at home, on the farm. She never had answered.

Victoria reached for the lettuce.

"Your hands," he said.

"Hmm?"

"The dirt."

Dirt covered her hands and lined her fingernails. Paul guessed she didn't know it soiled her shirt and jeans as well.

"Yes, of course."

She soaped her hands and began scrubbing them with a fingernail brush she kept by the sink for just such occasions. She scrubbed with vehemence, as she always did, trying to rid all traces of dirt from her skin. Sometimes she scrubbed long after he was able to see any remaining dirt.

Paul gathered silverware and plates and began setting the table. Anything to keep himself in her orbit a little longer.

The doorbell rang. Victoria cast a puzzled glance at Paul. He went to answer it. On the other side of the door, he found Rick Bahr.

"Anna thinks she left her purse in your study."

Paul urged him in. "Come in. Too cold to wait outside."

In the corner of the study, they found the purse. "Can't believe she left it," Rick said. "She can't go anywhere without it."

"Grief can turn a person around," Paul said. "Tell her Victoria and I have both been through this, if she wants to talk."

"That cliché about time and healing," Rick said. "I know that's true from when my own father passed." He met Paul's eyes. "Time wears away the rough edges. It makes all kinds of things easier." He headed back to the car.

When Paul's father had passed away eight months ago, Victoria had saved him. She sat with him in his office, day after day, and let him talk. She went with him to the funeral parlor and stood beside him throughout the funeral and the reception afterwards. She understood his loss. That was the beginning of their courtship.

As they dated, Paul held her hand or kissed her goodnight, but no more. It seemed no small miracle that she wanted to spend time with him.

When he proposed, in the front seat of his car, she hadn't responded until he touched her shoulder. "I don't think I'll make a good minister's wife," she said. She wouldn't meet his eyes. When he asked why not, she leaned her head against the window and stared out into the night. "I'm not a virgin."

He had taken her in his arms that night and whispered, "I know. I know," against her hair as he held her.

From first date to marriage took only four months. He hadn't touched her again until their wedding night. He still awoke in the middle of the night, in a cold sweat, filled with the urge to get down on his knees before her and beg her forgiveness for that one reckless night.

Paul watched Victoria shred lettuce and slice tomatoes. He went to her and put his hand on the curve of her hip. She inhaled sharply and closed her eyes. Beneath her rough cotton blouse, he felt her muscles tense.

"Let me help," he said.

She let her breath escape and her body relax, and she nodded. She handed him the lettuce.

Paul watched her hair tangle and shift over her back as she worked. She tucked her hair behind her ear and glanced at him.

"What is it?" she asked.

His chest began to tighten, restricting his breath. He saw the hesitation in her eyes and the guarded aspect returning to her face. Why did he feel as if he would never get beyond that reserve?

He shook it off. She was right there next to him. She was here, just as she had been from the day they met. The future stretched ahead of them, full of possibility, and time. That was all he and Victoria needed. Time.

The above selection features characters from Jeanmarie "Teri" Meadowcroft's novel in progress, In That Quiet Earth.

Over the Fence
Charlene Pollano

Every summer
my former neighbor
comes to visit by the shore;
our chance to recapture
times we shared
over the fence.
New babies,
how to heal diaper rash.
How she could move into a house
where another woman ran off, leaving
ravaged husband and daughters behind.
How I moved on after my husband left.
All over coffee, tears, and the fence.

Now, all it will take
after another year
is to sit on the porch swing
together, over coffee.
Talking of grown kids
and wishing we were back again,
over the fence.

Travelers to Sedona:
A Spiritual Adventure
Christine Parker

I could feel them. Twenty or so practically dancing at my feet. Not exactly dancing, but the power they emitted felt like they might start doing their own version of the polka any minute. Actually, I knew they had danced here. Right in this very spot. They were a merry group. No cares, really. Except, it was people like me they had to check out

I wasn't just your ordinary tourist, they knew that. If I had been, I wouldn't have known they were there. I had been hoping to find them. That was part of the plot. Find the little people. See past the obvious.

Low branches hung over my head. A few boulders sat throughout the small clearing that bordered on a creek. Scattered cactus gave way to the mountain next to this canyon.

Silence filled the air. It was as if they were waiting to see what I would do. What had I interrupted?

Nothing had prepared me for what to do if I came upon these ancients. It was just me and my imagination. Or theirs.

I knew one thing.

Anything can happen at a vortex.

This piece is the prologue to Christine Parker's work in progress, Travelers to Sedona: A Spiritual Adventure.

Mutiny
Georgia Ann Mullen

Maggie decided to rebel. Not a barefaced, tongue-sticking out, "I'm gonna do it anyway" defiance. She wasn't stupid. Her rebellion would be secret. Her family would never know she touched a Negro. At ten, Maggie believed everything her parents told her, except this: she didn't believe there was anything bad about black people.

In 1959 Maggie's parents and grandmother didn't shout their dislike of Negroes. They were sneaky. Grandma Stefi dropped her voice when she mentioned, "those black ones" even mouthing the word "black" as if it were a dirty word. Maggie's mother, Estelle, a registered nurse, did the same miming with words like "cancer" and "pregnant."

Still, Maggie was no stranger to the word "nigger," a stinger her father, Roland, and his male neighbors tossed under their breath as they sat around shootin' the breeze at the picnic table. Rolly used to dig ditches for a Cleveland utility company alongside other unskilled white Americans and immigrants from countries such as Poland and Hungary. He'd never mentioned colored ditch diggers, but by the way he joked about certain men, Maggie guessed a few got muddy, same as him. Now he drove a company truck and answered to "Chief," while passing 'round the feeling he was better than those white foreigners and black men he left swinging shovels in the trenches.

Comments about "those black ones" confused Maggie. Every Sunday and Holy Day, Estelle and Rolly dragged the family to church, where the message was, to Maggie's ears, that God loved everybody. She felt good when Estelle dropped a dollar in the extra basket for missions in Africa.

Maggie's church demanded that she sit through Mass every morning before walking across the parking lot to the parochial school, where catechism was the first class of the day. "Who is God?" the black-robed nun intoned. "God is the creator of all things," the blue-uniformed students sing-songed in reply. That response ignited a string of memorized mumblings that rolled off their young tongues like stray beads off a broken rosary.

So, if God loved everybody, and missionaries were swatting mosquitoes and eating watery rice while trying to save black African heathens, why weren't there any colored kids in her school? Maggie wondered if she was the only one paying attention.

"The blacks, they smell different," Grandma explained.

"What do they smell like?" Maggie asked.

Grandma Stefi grimaced. Shrugged. She couldn't pinpoint it. Testing Grandma's opinion, Maggie sniffed cautiously when passing a black man or woman on the street but didn't notice anything foul.

In addition to not sniffing coloreds, Grandma held tight to her pocketbook. "When I wait for the bus downtown—where there's a lot of those black ones—I hold it like this," and she demonstrated gripping her handbag between her arm and chest.

One day she mentioned a new employee at the dress factory where she worked. "They put the colored lady on piecework. She goes through her stack of collars in no time." Maggie wondered if that was a compliment or if Grandma was worried she couldn't keep up. She wondered if Grandma knew the colored lady's name.

The way her family talked about Negroes embarrassed Maggie. Made her feel sorry for black people. To her, "those coloreds were interesting. They came in not only different lengths and weights as did whites but also in a range of shades, hues and tones. They were colorful in the best definitions of the word. Rich. Vivid. Vibrant.

Maggie had few chances to study black people's habits and didn't think white adults did either. Her relatives and neighbors might work with a few Negroes, but their neighborhood was far from the streets closer to downtown where she was told "the black ones" lived. The only black people Maggie saw were on the bus and in stores doing the same things white people did. Buying dress fabric or plastic drink glasses at Woolworth's. Pushing baby carriages through drug store aisles, searching for Band-Aids and cotton balls. Their babies had round cheeks and runny noses same as white babies.

"They're always trying to touch us," Rolly told his neighbor one day. "Looking for an excuse to shake hands."

Men always shook hands, Maggie thought. Why would a white man not shake a black man's hand? What was so different about them? So strange? So dangerous? The message was sinking in that Maggie should stay away from colored people. Not touch them. But what would happen if she did? Would she get sick? Grow warts? Turn brown?

Maggie looked up from her homework. "Mom, did you ever touch a colored person?"

Estelle rolled her eyes toward the ceiling, shook her head slowly and mimed, "No." Maggie found this hard to believe. Her mother was a nurse on the children's floor. Maggie was certain black kids got sick. But she let it slide.

The next day, Maggie asked Grandma Stefi the same question and watched her stop dead for a good three seconds before continuing to wipe down the stove, speechless.

Despite these efforts to warn her away from "those black ones," Maggie wasn't getting the message. She decided the only way to find out what would happen, if she touched a black person, was to touch one.

This was difficult. She had no opportunity to hug a colored woman or brush up against a black kid during a recess game of dodge ball in her all-white school. And she couldn't just reach out and touch someone with black skin walking past her in the department store. Maggie was stumped.

Until she remembered the bus drivers. Maggie was allowed to ride the bus alone on Saturday mornings to her piano lesson. The bus driver was always the same, a chunky man with oak-toned skin that didn't contrast well with his tight, iron gray uniform. Brown hair, too short to be what Grandma called "kinky," covered enough of his head to save him from being tagged "Cue Ball." Funny, Maggie never heard the word "kinky" used to describe anything but black people's hair. This chubby, balding, brown-skinned bus driver didn't speak to or joke with the riders, but only called out street names as the bus approached the stop. "Watch your step," he'd say softly, pulling the lever to open the door.

Maggie's rebellion would occur immediately upon entering the bus. Every Saturday she climbed the two steep steps and dropped her dime into the glass and metal coin box. Fare for kids her age was ten cents. If she had a quarter, she gave it to the driver and he placed it in a coin dispenser and gave her back two dimes and a nickel. Then she put her dime in the coin box and heard the thin, ten-cent clink as it hit the heavier quarters, fifty-cent pieces and nest of dimes piled at the bottom. Until now, she'd been mindful to keep her skin away from his.

45

On the particular Saturday of Maggie's rebellion, she hoped to get a quarter and need change, but instead Estelle gave her two dimes, one for the return trip. This thwarted Maggie's plan and she pondered her problem as she walked to the bus stop.

Ten minutes later, heart prancing with excitement, Maggie watched the bus approach. She'd figured a way out of her dime dilemma. She was going to touch a Negro—consequences be damned.

With its usual squeal of brakes, the bus pulled to a halt, and its folding door opened with a gasp and a whoosh. Two adults waiting with her stepped forward. Maggie's excitement melted, replaced by a twinge in her chest that felt almost painful. Would the woman think Maggie wicked? Would the man toss what Estelle called a "dirty look?" A stinking cloud of exhaust from the bus's tailpipe swirled around her. If she lost her nerve, turned and left, she'd miss her music lesson and that wouldn't be good.

"Watch your step," the velvet-voiced bus driver called.

The woman entered first, the man behind her. Maggie exhaled. She wouldn't have to deal with their scorn after all.

She climbed onto the bus and stepped to the coin box. Swallowed hard. This was it.

Instead of dropping her dime into the box, Maggie handed it to the driver. As her thumb and index finger deposited the dime into his upturned hand, she let her little finger touch his skin.

Seeing a dime, the driver looked up in surprise. But Maggie was already walking down the aisle, the touch of his tan palm heavy on the tip of her pinky. When her dime clinked into the glass and metal box, she couldn't help smiling.

Holy moly! She'd touched a Negro. And nothing happened. No itching or burning sensation like ads on TV warned about bad rashes.

Her little finger didn't cramp, not even temporarily. Her skin wasn't even smudged. Of course, she'd have to wait a few days to see if some dread disease attacked her system, but she felt pretty safe.

When the bus arrived at the piano studio, Maggie walked boldly past the driver, not looking at him but wondering if he remembered her—the brave, white girl—just ten years old—who dared to touch his hand.

Maggie's joy lasted the entire half-hour music lesson. Every few seconds she lifted her right pinky off the keys and admired it. This was the finger, small, slim and white that proved her relatives wrong. A white person could touch a black person and live to tell the tale.

A different colored man drove the return bus home, but Maggie tossed her ten cents into the box, it not being necessary to repeat the challenge. She had pulled off the greatest coup of her ten years— white to black, pinky to palm.

At age ten, on a summer day, Maggie had touched a Negro.

Big Pig Problems
Christine Parker

Hot dog, it's hog time in North Carolina. Seems like the big fuss is the borough smell in Tarboro. You know, the I-40 hog farm smell that could just attack your nose on a Sunday afternoon drive. But the swine smell is not the only issue of great concern to the populace. Probably, more importantly, it's the ground water contamination. Now that's ser-i-ous!

Pig pollution from the billion-dollar industry of the 3,500 hog farmers in North Carolina is deadly serious. The farm factories get pretty ugly with pig poop running and ruining our land. The slaughtering of 15,000 to 20,000 swine per month just makes you want to throw up your bacon.

Shame on Bubba for putting his cute piglets in overcrowded pigpens where they get sick. Antibiotics needed for Penny the Pig are pickled into the food chain for Penny the person.

The good news, however, is that in 2012 the pig police fined one hog operator for dumping 324,000 gallons of hog waste into the Waccamaw River. Will we get sausage at the Piggly Wiggly that says "Pollution-Free?"

It is a wretched dilemma. Porky Pig or clear drinking water. Shortsighted selfishness or long-term solutions. Soon we'll all be buying Perrier water, not just for our car rides on the I-40, but probably to run it through our taps.

As they say in the South, "That do beat all."

The Weight of Grief
Jeanmarie "Teri" Meadowcroft

It drags down
The undead corpse,
The one left behind.
Anchors the living
To the sandy white floor,
Beneath
A sea of weary water.

Hot lead
In the elbows,
The ache of rotting timber.
Cartilage,
The agony of sand
Gritting between bone,
Swelling with time
And sea water sadness.

An entire ocean
Pressing down;
The weight of an ocean,
And all of heaven above.

Reflections on Spirituality
Charlene Pollano

I've realized half of me is often missing; kind of like I lost one shoe of a favorite pair. I'm not always aware of when it happens, but it affects many things: my daily quality of life, my career, my creative life and, most of all, my spiritual life. Here's how I figure it. The shoe I have possession of is my active life, the one I live every day—the "active" self.

But then there's that other half I have worked on cultivating through writing: the "reflective" self—the one that captures my feelings and beliefs about my "active" self. An awareness of myself within my own existence, or better, a form of spiritual journey I have embarked upon to interpret the meaning of this unique life I've been given.

When I do morning pages or journal writing, I sort through my actions, events, interactions with people in my life, and I sift it so it settles lightly into some kind of understanding. This is the shoe I often lose. It's important for me to monitor when I begin to lose touch with my reflective self, my spiritual being. I go on the hunt for that other favorite shoe, drag it out from under the bed or from the dark corner of the closet, shine it up and wear it so the pair is together.

Writing helps me greet myself on a deeper level. It is a ritual that, if practiced, helps rekindle my spirit. I think it's probably the best way for me to dig deep toward spirituality. It centers me and helps me listen to my inner voice. I feel more solid when I write, and

I am in search of a higher self. Also, finding my center is important in the midst of life's chaos. I can reach a point of centeredness but not maintain it—at work, especially.

Living my life on different levels is another way of looking at this splitting of my "being" in the world. At times I realize I have settled onto one floor of my life when I used to ride the elevator freely between levels. In the past, when my elevator remained stuck in the lobby, it usually signaled a transition period. It's hard to sit with these moments and trust the journey is going to bring me somewhere new, even though I am a person who believes in faith and the power of human beings to rise above. My career as a counselor—a witness to other people's sorrows—has brought much cynicism into my life, and I have had great difficulty tempering this cynicism with compassion. I remain a work in progress. Also, my own mid-life changes influence me, and I look inward for the definition of spirituality, and not in the ritual of religion.

I continually try to renew my faith and trust in the world and people. It means I'm always hunting for that other shoe! The journey to find it may lead me out of perceived order and into disorder. Disorder can be internal or external. My individual external life is not often disordered, but my internal state feels that way. People remind me life is neither ordered nor disordered: it just is. Life happens, but we interpret life events, and what we grant them for meanings is how we build our lives. This is where writing becomes so important. It's the opportunity to take a second look at certain events and cast special meaning on them.

I read a quote somewhere, "Be patient toward all that is unsolved in your heart…"

As a person in mid-life, what remains unsolved? I think all of my losses lie like stones in the bottom of my heart. But unsolved? There are burdens, but no mysteries as I reflect back. Sometimes the burdens weigh me down and prevent my spiritual life from unfolding. Casting off burdens from the past—consciously I've done so, but they are still lodged in my heart, or maybe my soul. Losses add up, but everyone has losses to overcome, some more than others. And some less, but of gigantic proportions. None of mine are gigantic, there's just a string of them dangling like broken Christmas lights.

It is what I don't understand and what I'm not comfortable with that drives my spiritual journey. Life has its shimmering moments when the world glistens with contentment, even joy. I have these moments, and that's perhaps when I'm lazy about my spirituality since I'm comfortable. My spirituality is fleeting, like the leaves I see skittering across the lawn. I need for it to be more grounded—solid—available to me at all times. Uppermost in my soul, at least. This is what I strive for through my writing. I love what Anne Lamott said in *Traveling Mercies*. She talks about her path of spirituality as happening in "fits and starts." Mine is more like stepping on land mines every few years! Blowing myself up, falling down to earth in pieces, regrouping and searching, then accepting there is a purpose. I need to learn about land mine detection. Or—how to fly!

This essay was published in the anthology Illuminations: Expressions of the Personal Spiritual Experience, *edited by Mark L. Tompkins and Jennifer McMahon, Celestial Arts, 2006.*

It's About Time
Nancy Gadzuk

"Get up!" Tony shook Vince's shoulders to wake him. "Get up." Tony shook harder, and Vince could smell the garlic on his dad's breath.

Vince opened his eyes. Tony's face was just inches away.

"Get dressed," Tony said. "We're leaving."

Vince had close to thirty years of experience with his dad, enough to do what he was told, even when it involved a seemingly ridiculous demand in the middle of the night. He struggled to pull himself out of his dream as he sat up in bed.

It was 2:18. By the time Vince had gotten dressed, he was fully awake. He followed his father to the garage.

"You drive," Tony said, as he handed him the keys.

"I don't see no good in the dark. Head for the Pike. *Fretta.*"

Vince took a hard right at Tony's command, then a left toward the highway.

As Vince headed up the entrance ramp to the New Jersey Turnpike, he heard a boom, an explosion behind him. Black smoke filled the rear view window, and Vince saw flames shooting from his old neighborhood. Tony spat *"buon riddance"* out the side window.

Life, as Vince Fantozzi knew it, had just ended. It was 2:27 A.M.

Somewhere in the Carolinas, Tony told Vince to turn east off Interstate 95 and head toward the ocean. He handed Vince a new driver's license and said, "Here. This is you now."

interlude

The license had Vince's picture on it, but he didn't recognize the name. Whatever Tony would give as a reason for the new identity was unlikely to be the truth, so Vince didn't even bother to ask.

Life in Jersey hadn't been that great for Vince, so he wasn't sorry to leave. He'd moved back home when his mother was sick, and he watched her waste away over agonizingly long months. He'd spent hours in the kitchen preparing foods he hoped she could eat. Nothing seemed to help her—not the chemo, not the minestrone, not even the amaretto ricotta pie.

After she died, Vince was ready to move on with his life. But he needed cash. And he made a mistake that cost him dearly.

The wigs had come all the way from South America. How was Vince supposed to know the genuine human hair would still be attached to genuine human heads when the shipment arrived at La Guardia? He'd trusted the wrong guy as a business partner.

Getting out of the wig fiasco required more than a little muscle from some of Tony's friends, and Tony never let Vince forget he owed him. Vince's entire life became devoted to doing whatever Tony wanted.

And that was just the way Tony liked it.

"Turn in here." Tony pointed to an ornate fountain cascading around three concrete dolphins in front of a sign advertising Royal Palm Breeze. He gave Vince a four-digit code to punch into the box at the gate, and the heavy steel gate swung open.

Tony had picked the Royal Palm Breeze community, he said, because he liked the palm trees and the vegetation. That was bunk, and Vince knew it. Tony liked the high brick wall and the gated entrance that kept outsiders outside.

Vince's life was not much different in Royal Palm Breeze than it had been in Jersey. Once a week, he would drive to Walmart with as many twenty dollar bills as Tony decided he'd need for groceries, and that was it. Most days Vince would take the long route home, pull the SUV into the Krispy Kreme drive-through and spend the change on an iced coffee, extra cream and sugar. That small sweet pleasure and his daily run, either through the neighborhood or on a treadmill in the garage, drowning out the mess his life had become with his iPod at full volume, became the high points of Vince's week.

He spent every afternoon preparing Tony's dinner, to be served promptly at 6 P.M.

"No eggs," Tony said firmly, "I don't want no eggs." He settled back in the lounge chair, facing his new 65-inch flat screen TV, and turned up the volume. He spoke loud enough that his voice carried into the kitchen.

Vince put the finishing touches on the frittata, carefully arranging prosciutto and roasted asparagus on top of the glistening yellow pie before putting it back in the oven.

"I don't want no eggs," Tony said again. Vince had gone to three stores before he found the low cholesterol, free-range, organic eggs with omega 3 that earlier in the day Tony'd insisted he wanted for dinner.

Vince opened the oven door and looked at the frittata browning under the broiler. Perfect. He slid it onto a platter, garnished it with parsley and cherry tomatoes, and carried it to the table.

"I don't want no eggs."

One of these days, Vince hoped Tony would get what he deserved instead of what he demanded.

Then Shirley and Jack moved in next door, and Vince finally got his wish.

Shirley had had an impressive amount of augmentative surgery in her forty-some years. In case anyone she met was unaware of it, she would bend down in front of them, shake just enough to start jiggling and say, "I don't know why, but men always seem to look at my chest."

Shirley's assets were not lost on either Tony or Vince, though Vince held out very little hope or interest in seeing much more of Shirley than what he'd enjoyed when she first introduced herself in the driveway, bending over to pick a non-existent leaf off the ground. She was wearing a form-fitting tank top with "A Hard Man Is Good to Find" emblazoned on the front.

Shirley's bathroom window was made of the rippled glass blocks that were supposed to blur images to the outside world. When she turned on the ceiling light and stood close to the glass blocks while showering, anyone on the outside could see Shirley's most prominent features clearly. The glass block window faced Tony's breakfast table, and he began savoring Shirley's shower along with his morning espresso.

After a week of watching, Tony invited Shirley and Jack to come for dinner.

Vince spent two days cleaning, making sauces, cleaning, rolling fresh pasta, cleaning, roasting peppers, and making fancy Italian pastries while Tony shouted orders at him.

The doorbell rang at exactly 5:45. Shirley wore a low-cut sundress and she leaned forward as she greeted Tony, jiggling ever so slightly. Vince stayed in the kitchen, stirring sauces and making sure the pasta didn't cook too long. He hadn't cooked for company since his mother died and he was looking forward to the opportunity.

He poured chunky sauce on the pasta and sprinkled pungent cheese over the entire bowl. A twist of the pepper grinder and he tasted it: delicious. He carried the steaming bowl into the dining room and set it on the table between a huge green salad and a basket of crusty bread.

"Okay, folks. Dinner's on." Vince sat down with a sigh of relief. Even Tony wouldn't be able to criticize this meal.

Jack picked up a big jug of red wine and started pouring as everyone passed the food around the table and began eating. Halfway through the bottle, Tony started talking. He told Shirley and Jack he'd been a successful banker in Jersey, that he'd made a killing there. He wanted to retire while he was ahead, he said, while he could enjoy some deep-sea fishing.

This was hogwash and Vince struggled to keep his mouth shut. Whatever "banking" Tony had done was not the kind one reported to the IRS. And while he may indeed have made a killing up north, it was certainly not the kind he was implying to his guests.

Vince got up and brought out a tray of pastries, oozing with whipped cream and shaved chocolate. Shirley grabbed two without taking her eyes off Tony.

It was close to midnight when Shirley and Jack stood up to leave. Shirley leaned so far over Tony she practically fell out of her sundress. Tony sat on his hands to keep from groping her.

The next day, Shirley took a second shower in the late afternoon. She did a slow motion dance in the water and Tony applauded quietly when she finished.

Over the next couple of weeks, Vince prepared dinner for Shirley and Jack almost every night. Once they went to Shirley and Jack's, but Shirley said she didn't like to cook. The meal she prepared was a testament to her lack of culinary skills.

Jack helped Vince in the kitchen rather than watch Tony and Shirley ogle each other. Jack wasn't much of a talker, and he watched to see how Vince made the pasta, the sauces, those desserts. While

Vince cooked, Shirley and Tony would disappear into Tony's bedroom, only emerging when the platters of food were set on the table.

One afternoon Tony seemed on edge, at a loss for words. Vince had never seen his father so uncomfortable. Finally Tony cleared his throat and said, "You gotta go."

"What?" Vince didn't understand.

Tony said it again. "You gotta go."

There was a light tap on the door, and Shirley came in dragging a huge suitcase. She giggled nervously when she saw Vince with his mouth hanging open.

"Here," Tony said. "You gonna need something to get started." Tony pulled a small wad of bills out of his pocket and tossed them to Vince. Shirley frowned when she saw the bills land in Vince's hands. "You too old to be hanging on me all the time anyway. Now get out of here." Tony turned away from Vince and picked up Shirley's suitcase.

Vince stared as Tony and Shirley moved down the hall. His stomach did a somersault when Tony's bedroom door slammed shut.

What the hell was going on? Had Tony just kicked him out of the house? Vince shook his head as if to remove imaginary cobwebs. Then he started moving.

He grabbed an empty plastic trash bag and filled it with some clothes, his running shoes, his toilet kit. It didn't take long. A framed picture of his mother, laughing and healthy looking, sat on the sideboard. He tucked it carefully between his T-shirts and headed for the door.

Jack was sitting at his kitchen table when Vince walked in.

"Hey," said Vince. "How you doing?"

Jack looked at him. "You want the truth?"

Vince nodded.

Jack drained his beer before speaking. "I feel pretty good, as a matter of fact. Shirley's a real piece of work. How about you?" He got two more bottles out of the refrigerator and handed one to Vince.

Vince took a long draught. The sharp cold helped him focus his thoughts. He realized he felt light, lighter than he had in several years.

"Great. I feel great." He was surprised by the truth of his words. He *did* feel great. "Tony's not all that easy to live with."

Jack nodded toward Vince's belongings. "You can throw that stuff in the front closet. Couch is yours as long as you want it."

They sat together in comfortable silence until it began to get dark. Shirley had always insisted on taking the leftovers home after dinner at Tony's, so they made a salad and reheated Vince's good sausage lasagna. Dinner without Tony tasted delicious.

Jack looked at his watch and said, "I rarely get a chance to watch, but they're showing reruns of *Murder, She Wrote* at 9 P.M. every weeknight this month."

Vince couldn't believe it. He loved *Murder, She Wrote*! This felt too good to be true. It *was* too good to be true, and Vince worried through the entire show.

As the credits rolled he asked, "How long do you think Shirley can last over there? Tony's one mean SOB. He's used to me waiting on him hand and foot. And he's lying about rolling in dough. He doesn't have any money. At least none that Shirley'd ever get her hands on."

"He doesn't have any money?" Jack frowned. "When she finds that out, she'll be back here in a heartbeat." He cracked his knuckles.

"And that'd put me back over there with Tony," Vince said.

They both thought hard for a minute.

interlude

Vince had learned a few things from his old man, and he sprang into action. He barked orders at Jack, and Jack jumped to follow them.

They didn't have much time. They worked quickly, quietly in the dark. Finally, they loaded Jack's Jeep and headed down the street, headlights dimmed until they turned the corner.

They drove out of Royal Palm Breeze, away from the glass block windows, away from the high wall, the steel gate across the entrance. Already the air smelled fresher.

They heard the boom, the loud explosion behind them. Billows of smoke filled the rear view window.

Vince glanced at the dashboard clock and smiled. It was 2:27 A.M.

Sweet.

The above is an excerpt from Nancy's 2013 novel, Moon Beach Magic, *published under the pseudonym Natasha Alexander.*

Bertha Blows
Christine Parker

Bertha, Big Bertha, now what will you do?
Topple a house, just give me a clue.
The eye of your fury headed my way
Causing house innards to be boarded all day.

I hurried and toiled as fast as I could
Scurrying to safety, just as one should.
Leaving the cottage before the waves came
Getting out of your path and not playing your game.

My first coastal hurricane I awaited with awe.
My sister declared you'll not laugh at all.
It was hard to convince me a storm such as you
Is more scary than any earthquake I knew.

Movement of earth needs no preparation.
I stand under doorways in expectation.
When moments go by and all is the same
I wonder why Easterners fear nature's vein.

So hurry on Bertha, I'm waiting for you.
Locked up indoors wondering what's new.
I sense the wind's scorn and see bushes sway
Stirred with anticipation of Bertha hitting today.

Make It About the Money
Nancy Gadzuk

August 2010

The heat index was 107 degrees. That's hot, even for August in the Carolinas. Alton the tree guy was cutting branches from the live oaks, and he looked ready for a break when I brought out some ice water.

He sat on the bumper of his truck and took a long slug before wiping the sweat off his face.

So I asked him, was he looking forward to hurricane season and some extra tree work afterward. He took another long drink before saying anything.

"Tell you what happens. There's a hurricane here and before the wind dies down–these guys show up from Arkansas, Alabama, Louisiana with their rigs.

"And they start hitting all the neighborhoods like this. I give you a quote for, say, two fifty, and this guy's right behind me saying 'I'll clear them trees for a hunnerd.'

"This guy's talking at you and talking at you and there's a bunch of guys setting in the back of his truck drinking Bud Light and eating pork rinds. Just setting there waiting.

"Then while he's cutting your trees and you think you're saving a buck, his guys are clearing out your garage, your truck, your toolbox. You don't even know it 'til they done gone and you never see 'em or your tools again.

"I don't say nothing when they come in. Them guys'd shut me down in a day if I talked, and it wouldn't be pretty how they do it.

"I just hope the folks what used me last year and the year before remember me and don't go with them other guys.

"I been here forever, and I ain't going nowhere. I'll be here tomorrow. But them guys? They be gone just as fast they clean you out.

"Nah, I don't like the hurricane business none."

He spat on the ground and started in on the BP oil spill. It was the middle of August and the well had been spewing oil since April.

"Now that BP thing coulda been fixed in five, mebbe six days." He talked fast–and with a lot of hand motions–about how you'd drill into a whosis and tap off the whatsis and it seemed to make sense.

Who knows? The guy had two big trucks, a cherry picker, three different sized front-end loaders, and tools spread out all down the street. He was a genius at maneuvering around branches and dropping limbs to the ground without breaking a sweat or the neighbor's fence. He might have been blowing more than hot air.

Still, here's when he really started talking sense: "You gotta make it about the money, y'know? Make it worth it to someone to fix the thing. Then someone'd figure out right quick how to plug the damn well.

"Tell ya, you got a tree up on top of, I don't care where–the Empire State Building–and you wanna pay." He pointed to his son, Dale. "Him and me'll figure out a way to get up there and cut the damn tree."

He held out his hand and rubbed his thumb across his fingertips.

"Make it about the money.

interlude

"We got a problem with beavers up at our farms and so the guy from the county comes out and asks me do I got any idea how to get rid of them beavers. I tell him, put a bounty on 'em.

"Put a bounty on 'em—ten, fifteen, twenty dollars a head—don't matter how much. Dale here and ten of his buddies'll be out there in a minute, and them beavers'll be gone by morning.

"It'll sound like World War II out there for a while, but by dawn next day them beavers'll be gone.

"I guarantee it."

He hitched up his pants and got back to work.

This piece was first published under the pseudonym Natasha Drew by The Dead Mule School of Southern Literature *in 2011. It was also a nominee for Best of the Net 2011.*

An 'Ole Scarlett Tale
Christine Parker

Bless my soul, Ashley,
You must love me.
I'd do anything for you.
I'd even cook
And have Mammy clean Tara.
I just don't understand
Your lack of interest.
What do you see in Melanie
That you don't see in me?

Pray tell, will I ever find
My Prince of Light?
I've done all I could.
I need God's strength
To go on and on.
To sow the field, pull the weeds,
Harvest the crop.
I've worked like a slave,
I've gotten rid of the Yankees.
What is to become of me?

I want the moon,
I seek the stars.
I need the beauty of Tara.
But Ashley loves another.

interlude

With this emptiness shall
I just marry "He'll Do?"
Because maybe
Love is never to be.
Perhaps it takes more than I've got
To get what I want.

It's not fair.
I should have listened to Papa.
He was right, you know,
Sometimes you can't have it all.
But that thought feels
Too painful to bear.
Oh, what shall I do?

Papa would say
That love not returned
Is not love at all.
That I must be brave.
And this too shall pass,
Just like the war.
Oh, it is too unbearable.

I have a creeping suspicion
He might just come around.
If only he could see me for my real self.
Oh, I do love him so.
But now,
My neck hurts, my bones ache.
I think I'll just go lie down for a while.
And think about this tomorrow.

Contributors

Marilyn Coyne began painting when she retired from her cruise business in Wrightsville Beach. Her painting "Japanese Garden House" won first place in the Brunswick County Senior Arts Contest and second place in the State Senior Arts Contest. Marilyn is inspired by the beauty of the North Carolina scenery. She lives in Hampstead, North Carolina with her husband, Robert Falk. Visit her on Facebook at Marilynspaintings.

Nancy Gadzuk writes contemporary fiction featuring quirky characters stumbling toward self-awareness, decent cannoli, and possibly, love. Her first novel, *Moon Beach Magic*, is written under the pseudonym Natasha Alexander. In earlier lifetimes, Nancy worked in publishing, taught at various levels from kindergarten through university, designed interactive video, attended theological school, and conducted ethnographic research in urban schools. If she's not writing, she's probably walking on the beach or singing. Please visit her Natasha Alexander persona at Goodreads or on her website: http://natasha.edcentric.org.

Jeanmarie "Teri" Meadowcroft received her MFA in Creative Writing from the University of North Carolina Wilmington in 2004. When she was fifteen, she adopted the nom e plume "Teri Raven." While she no longer writes under an alias, the nickname "Teri" stuck. She is currently at work on her novel, *In That Quiet Earth*, a modern retelling of *Wuthering Heights*.

Georgia Ann Mullen is the author of two historical fiction novels: *A Shocking & Unnatural Incident* and *Wixumlee Is My Salvation*. Her work in progress, tentatively titled *Worse than Dead*, draws on the trauma of human trafficking—black slaves, white females and children—in the tumultuous decade before the Civil War. Georgia is a former journalist who blogs about modern day slavery and women's rights at www.georgiamullen.com. She can be found on Facebook at Historical Fiction by Georgia Ann Mullen. When not writing, Georgia enjoys kayaking, sitting at sea turtle nests, and strumming her ukulele.

Christine Parker, MS, is the author of *Patient Notes,* a calendar that helps bridge the communication gap between patient, physicians and caregivers. Christine left California after twenty years to return to her home state, North Carolina. She shares her collective prose while poking a little fun at the South.

Charlene Pollano has published short stories and essays in literary journals and anthologies and is the co-author of *A Group of One's Own: Nurturing the Woman Writer.* (A second edition is in the planning stages.) She is working on a final revision of her novel, *I Almost Remember,* which was second runner-up in the Three

Oaks Prize for Fiction. A New Hampshire native who retired to North Carolina, Charlene is enjoying southern culture, including collards, oysters, and shrimp and grits.